IMAGES
of America

BUILDING WASHINGTON
NATIONAL CATHEDRAL

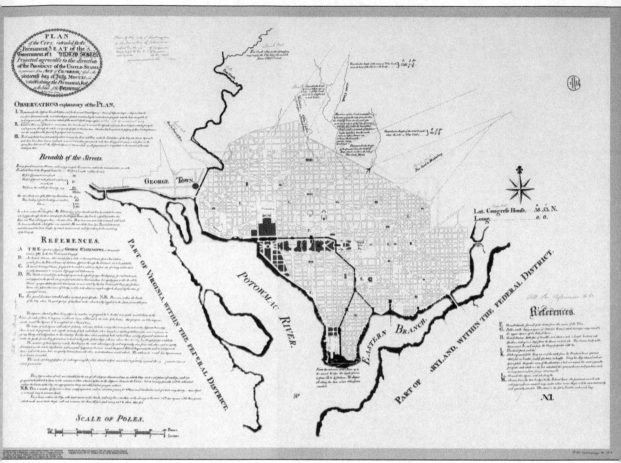

L'Enfant's Suggestion. In the references section of his 1791 plan for the city of Washington, city planner Pierre L'Enfant suggested a particular building be constructed at Eighth and F Streets, NW: "This church is intended for national purposes, such as public prayer, thanksgivings, funeral orations, etc., and assigned to the special use of no particular sect or denomination, but equally open to all." (Library of Congress [LOC].)

On the Cover: Building Washington National Cathedral took 83 years, from September 29, 1907, to September 29, 1990. In a photograph taken 16 years into the longest-running construction project in the history of Washington, DC, one worker with a wheelbarrow atop the rising wall of St. Mary's Chapel gives scale to the magnitude of the enterprise. (Washington National Cathedral [WNC].)

IMAGES
of America

BUILDING WASHINGTON
NATIONAL CATHEDRAL

R. Andrew Bittner

ARCADIA
PUBLISHING

Published by Arcadia Publishing
Charleston, South Carolina

Library of Congress Control Number: 2015950109

For all general information, please contact Arcadia Publishing:
Telephone 843-853-2070
Fax 843-853-0044
E-mail sales@arcadiapublishing.com
For customer service and orders:
Toll-Free 1-888-313-2665

Visit us on the Internet at www.arcadiapublishing.com

This book is dedicated to the memory of my dear friend Donna Sappe Hrozencik. She was my biggest fan, ready "first reader," constant encouragement, and passed away during the writing of this book.

CONTENTS

ACKNOWLEDGMENTS

Special thanks are due to those without whose help this book would not have happened: Robert Sokol, chief operating officer at Washington National Cathedral, green-lighted the project and provided constant support. Craig Stapert and Diane Ney, the cathedral's director of communications and archivist, allowed access and provided guidance through two great photographic collections that were essential to going forward.

Thanks go to Clift A. Seferlis, for his invaluable support; Donovan Marks, for introducing me to the cathedral communication department's digital photograph archive; Matthew Gilmore, for helping me find the L'Enfant map; Susan Jensen, for providing images that proved valuable in the end; and my Saturday docent team, for their encouragement and ready opinions.

Last, I would like to thank all the wonderful people who built or have served Washington National Cathedral over the years. I have tried to tell their story faithfully, albeit briefly. The 191 photographs in this volume were selected from over 1,000 images collected to tell this story. Any truly comprehensive photographic record of the construction of Washington National Cathedral would have taken many, many more volumes. I did my best.

INTRODUCTION

When Maj. Pierre L'Enfant was commissioned to lay out the United States' new capital city, Washington, in the District of Columbia, he allowed space on one of his early plans, and in the heart of the city, for "a great church for national purposes." That much we know, but from there the stories become a matter of lore and conjecture. Some suggest the choice to include such a church was the result of a conversation between L'Enfant and Pres. George Washington. Fewer, but nonetheless some, have suggested this conversation may have taken place on the highest point overlooking the site for the future city, a hill that would become known as Mount St. Alban. L'Enfant's "great church" did not survive to the city's final plan. If it had, the separation of church and state would have ensured the federal government could not have built it. A building now known as the Old Patent Office was built on the proposed site of L'Enfant's great church.

Almost 100 years later, prominent leaders in the Episcopal Church in the United States decided they wanted a monumental church building to serve the nation and represent the Episcopal denomination nationally. The logical location for such a church would be in the nation's capital city, and Pierre L'Enfant's "great church for national purposes" suggestion, dormant for nearly a century, was raised again as part of the Episcopal cathedral concept. Properly rendered, maybe the new Episcopal cathedral could also answer L'Enfant's vision. At the time, the Episcopal churches in Washington, DC, were part of that group of churches known as the Episcopal Diocese of Maryland. The Episcopal Diocese of Maryland already had plans to build its cathedral, the seat for the diocesan bishop, in Baltimore. The suggestion of creating a Washington, DC, diocese out of a portion of the Maryland diocese was not a new one, but the discussion of a great church, a national Episcopal cathedral in Washington, brought the Episcopal Diocese of Washington, DC, with the new cathedral as its seat, into being.

As the notion of the great Episcopal cathedral developed, important decisions were made. It was decided that although the new church building would be the seat of the Episcopal denomination in America and the seat of the new Episcopal Diocese of Washington, it would not receive direct funding from either of these organizations and would thus not be answerable, at the end of any given day, to the political budgeting and funding processes of a larger church body. The new cathedral, the Cathedral Church of St. Peter and St. Paul, would be built under the auspices of a private foundation, the Protestant Episcopal Cathedral Foundation, and entirely from private gifts and donations.

The Protestant Episcopal Cathedral Foundation was chartered on January 6, 1893, in the city of Washington, DC. The charter was provided by Congress and signed by Pres. Benjamin Harrison. This can be a confusing truth, because it can seem the government decided to build a big church. In reality, the Protestant Episcopal Cathedral Foundation was chartered, as are most nonprofit organizations in the United States, through the local government (city or county councils) over the signature of the local elected executive (mayor, county executive, and so forth). It just so happens, at that time in its history, the local government for Washington, DC, was a committee in Congress, and the de facto local executive was the sitting president of the United States.

On March 25, 1896, the Right Reverend Henry Yates Satterlee was consecrated as first bishop of the new Episcopal Diocese of Washington. The consecration took place in New York. The new diocese would include the Protestant Episcopal churches located within the District of Columbia and Montgomery, Prince George's, Charles, and St. Mary's Counties in Maryland. While the churches of the new diocese would be his primary responsibility, it was also clear the new cathedral was a driving factor in the entire movement.

Fundraising for the new cathedral commenced, and the first priority was finding a site for the church. While many potential sites were considered, it was finally decided to purchase a 58-acre tract of land in northwest Washington, which included Mount St. Alban, the highest point overlooking the federal city. The site was considered distant from the city, but it was large, relatively affordable, occupied a commanding position on the city's horizon, and offered a location that could properly accommodate a very large church building on the traditional west-to-east orientation.

In 1898, the Mount St. Alban property was purchased, incurring a debt of $245,000, on which Bishop Satterlee made personal assurances. The property was adjacent to and mostly surrounding St. Alban's Parish, an Episcopal church built over 40 years earlier. The charter of the Protestant Episcopal Cathedral Foundation states that the goals of the organization include the promotion of matters of religion, education, and charity. The cathedral property, referred to as "the Close," would eventually be home to four schools. They are National Cathedral School for Girls, St. Albans School for Boys, Beauvoir Elementary School, and the College of Preachers. The National Cathedral School for Girls would be the first, opening in October 1900.

In the years before Henry Yates Satterlee was consecrated as the bishop of Washington, there was considerable debate over the architectural style of the new cathedral. Some of the cathedral's founders favored the medieval Gothic style, while others favored a Classical Renaissance style. Eventually, the Classical Renaissance style was chosen, and architect Ernest Flagg was invited to submit a design. Flagg's plan offered a French Beaux-Arts style domed building, which resembled, to some degree or another, both St. Paul's Cathedral in London and St. Peter's Basilica in Vatican City. Then Satterlee became bishop and lent the weight of his opinion to those still favoring a Gothic cathedral. He had called Gothic "God's style," firmly believed he had popular opinion on his side, and felt no other architectural style could inspire religious feeling to nearly the same degree.

Although Ernest Flagg had been awarded the contract for both the cathedral and the first building at the National Cathedral School for Girls, his reputation began to slip as a result of notable cost overruns on other projects. When his proposal for the National Cathedral School's Hearst Hall came in at double the amount budgeted, both of his cathedral projects—the church and the school—were taken from him. This was exactly the kind of break needed by those still advocating the Gothic style. One of Bishop Satterlee's noteworthy attributes was his ability to work behind the scenes, and shortly after the Mount St. Alban property was paid off, in 1905, it was decided, with little noise or fanfare, the architectural style would be English Gothic. Bishop Satterlee chose acclaimed Gothic Revival architects George Frederick Bodley and Henry Vaughan to design the new cathedral, and after those plans were approved, the foundation stone for Washington's National Cathedral—the Cathedral Church of St. Peter and St. Paul—was set on September 29, 1907.

One

1891–1910

PEACE CROSS. On October 23, 1898, after the cessation of hostilities in the Spanish-American War but before the ratification of the Treaty of Paris, Washington National Cathedral's founders dedicated a Peace Cross on their newly acquired Mount St. Alban property. Pres. William McKinley attended the service dedicating that cross, which faces the Capitol and celebrates both the founding of the cathedral and the end of the war. (LOC.)

A Big Domed Church. The first plan for the Washington National Cathedral was a large Classical Renaissance–style church, designed by Ernest Flagg. The style and the plan were chosen by an illustrious committee of important church leaders, as well as highly regarded artists, architects, landscape architects, and other relevant experts. However, there were still powerful individuals who were seeing things differently; favoring the English Gothic architectural style. Flagg was also asked to submit a plan for the new National Cathedral School for Girls. The plan Flagg delivered for the school almost doubled the proposed budget for that building. Flagg and his plan for the cathedral were out. (WNC.)

BISHOP SATTERLEE. Henry Yates Satterlee was born in New York City in 1843, educated at Columbia University and the General Theological Seminary, and ordained an Episcopal priest in 1867. On March 26, 1896, after serving as rector of New York City's Calvary Church for 14 years, Satterlee was consecrated as the first bishop of a new Episcopal Diocese of Washington, DC, the very existence of which seemed to be predicated, at least in part, on plans to construct Washington National Cathedral. Satterlee felt that the Gothic style was the one and only style suitable for a church building of this magnitude and importance. (WNC.)

PHILIP HUBERT FROHMAN. Philip Hubert Frohman was born in 1887, the grandson of renowned architect Philip Hubert. This early childhood photograph suggests a strong family affinity for the architectural profession. Around the age of seven, Frohman became aware of the Episcopal Church's plans to build a great Classical Renaissance–style cathedral in Washington, DC. Immediately, he decided the new cathedral needed to be Gothic in architectural style and that he wanted to be its architect. He declared his intent to become a church builder at 11. As a student at Throop Polytechnic, he designed his first fully functional home at the age of 14 and achieved his architectural degree at 16. At the age of 20, he became the youngest person to ever receive an architectural license in California. By his first visit to Washington, at age 27, the architectural style of the new cathedral had been changed to Gothic and construction was underway. At the age of 34, Frohman signed the contract that would make him Washington National Cathedral's chief architect for over 50 years. (WNC.)

GEORGE FREDERICK BODLEY AND
HENRY VAUGHAN. When it was
decided the architectural style of
Washington National Cathedral
would be English Gothic, Bishop
Henry Yates Satterlee chose an
eminent British Gothic Revivalist,
George Frederick Bodley (right), as
the cathedral's primary architect,
supported by another noteworthy
Gothic Revival–style architect, Henry
Vaughan (below). While Bodley is
credited with the original drawings
for the new Gothic church building,
he would pass away within one month
of the setting of the cathedral's
foundation stone. Vaughan would
continue to work as the cathedral's sole
architect, refining and implementing
Bodley's plans until own death in 1917.
The cathedral's first chapel, Bethlehem
Chapel, is considered a masterwork
of Vaughan's career. (Both, WNC.)

THE FOUNDATION STONE. Bishop Henry Yates Satterlee knew the Gothic architectural style had its roots in medieval Roman Catholic Europe and that his new American Protestant Gothic cathedral might lack for any experience similar to the Roman Catholic regard and veneration of relics. Satterlee's solution was to bring stones from thought-provoking locations in religious, American, or even world history and place them in important locations throughout the church. The cathedral's foundation stone was the first of many such stones. A fieldstone was brought from a sheep field near Bethlehem and inscribed with the cathedral's founding statement, "The Word was made flesh, and dwelt among us." The Bethlehem stone was then set into a larger piece of American granite, on which the cathedral's official name, the Cathedral Church of St. Peter and St. Paul, was carved, along with the cathedral's founding day, the Feast of St. Michael and All Angels, and year, AD 1907. (WNC.)

FOUNDATION STONE SERVICE. On September 29, 1907, the Feast of St. Michael and All Angels, over 10,000 people gathered on Mount St. Alban to witness the dedication of Washington National Cathedral's foundation stone. Although the future building site was still mostly wooded hilltop, the service's processional (above) came from west to east, down the length of what would eventually be the cathedral's center aisle. The foundation stone (below) was placed at the east end of the cathedral's footprint-to-be, with a VIP grandstand beyond. In attendance in the grandstand are Pres. Theodore Roosevelt, Bishop Henry Yates Satterlee, architect Henry Vaughan, Adm. George Dewey, and a long list of bishops and clergy from across the country and around the world. (Both, WNC.)

FIRST CONSTRUCTION PHOTOGRAPH. Construction at Washington National Cathedral began with excavation for the foundations of Bethlehem Chapel. At the time, Bethlehem Chapel was the only worship space planned for the cathedral's lower level. The foundation stone stands in protective enclosure to the left. With the exception of the clothing, the style of mule-drawn wagon, and one motorized cement mixer, there is little in this photograph to suggest this image is from the 20th century. (WNC.)

BISHOP ALFRED HARDING. Following the death of Bishop Henry Yates Satterlee in March 1908, Rev. Alfred Harding was elected and consecrated to the office of bishop of Washington. With construction in progress, there would soon be a building to administer. Harding initiated the position and office of dean of Washington National Cathedral. He would also serve in that role until 1916. (WNC.)

BETHLEHEM CHAPEL FOUNDATIONS. With the foundation stone still protected in its enclosure, the foundations of Bethlehem Chapel are growing. Using unreinforced concrete, the foundations for this chapel and this end of the building would, in some places, be as much as 20 feet from bottom to top. Even at this early stage, the complexity of a great church building site is becoming apparent. (WNC.)

BELOW BETHLEHEM CHAPEL. From down in the construction of Bethlehem Chapel's foundations, the scale of the project becomes readily apparent, as does the lack of any occupational-safety organization specifying the shoring of what must be almost 20 feet of dirt wall. (WNC.)

BETHLEHEM CHAPEL CORNERSTONE. By November 1, 1910, the foundations of Bethlehem Chapel were complete, and the cathedral community was ready to celebrate the setting of that chapel's cornerstone and the first rising of the cathedral. Bishop Alfred Harding presided at the service. Henry Yates Satterlee II, grandson of the late Bishop Henry Yates Satterlee, wielded the ceremonial trowel. Bethlehem Chapel would be dedicated to the memory of Bishop Satterlee, and thus, the Bethlehem Chapel cornerstone would also serve as a time capsule, containing items of contemporary interest such as then-current newspapers as well as images of Bishop Satterlee and items related to his life and career. (WNC.)

Two

1911–1920

THE RISING WALLS OF THE APSE. The new decade would bring about the building of the east end of Washington National Cathedral, the apse. As the walls of the apse begin to rise on top of Bethlehem Chapel, the flying buttresses that will eventually support the main apse vault (ceiling) rise along with them. Much higher, they will reach across arches to resist the vault's outward thrust. (Photograph by Commercial Photo Inc., WNC.)

BETHLEHEM CHAPEL. Completed, opened, and dedicated in the spring of 1912, Bethlehem Chapel would eventually become the final resting place of Bishop Henry Yates Satterlee and Adm. George Dewey. On seeing it, in 1914, Philip Hubert Frohman would declare Bethelehem Chapel to be the most pleasing example of Gothic architecture in North America. From the completion of this chapel forward, there would be daily worship services held inside the cathedral building. (Author's collection.)

PRESIDENT WILSON AND FRANCIS BOWES SAYRE JR. On January 17, 1915, Jessie Woodrow Wilson Sayre, Pres. Woodrow Wilson's daughter, gave birth to a son, Francis Bowes Sayre Jr., at the White House. With time, both President Wilson and his grandson would become important figures in the history of Washington National Cathedral. (Photograph by Harris & Ewing, LOC.)

DEAN BRATENAHL. By 1916, Bishop Alfred Harding and Washington National Cathedral's chapter, the cathedral's governing board, created the independent office of cathedral dean. The first person filling the new role would be the Very Reverend Carl George Fitch Bratenahl, former rector of St. Albans Episcopal Parish, the cathedral's neighbor. Bratenahl would be responsible for most of the major iconographic themes eventually played out in the cathedral's art. (WNC.)

THE VESTRY (FLOWER ROOM) VAULT. From beginning to end, the techniques used to build Washington National Cathedral were centuries and sometimes millennia old. The process used to set the broad groin vault of the cathedral's vestry is among the older: Build a wooden framework, or falsework, shaped like the intended ceiling, and fit stones tightly across the top; pull out the falsework, and let gravity take over. (WNC.)

21

APSE TRIFORIUM. In the most common form for Gothic great-church architecture, the interior elevation is dominated by three horizontal levels. The lowest is a tall arcade of arches; the middle, the triforium, is a low band of smaller, shorter arches; and the highest is the tall clerestory arches containing the clerestory windows. While a regular triforium has a significant open space behind the arches, Washington National Cathedral's apse triforium is a false triforium, with no space behind. (WNC.)

FIRST FLYING BUTTRESSES. By the spring of 1917, the apse at Washington National Cathedral had been built to the clerestory level. With the inner and outer arches of the clerestory completed and the wall rising between, the flying buttress, otherwise separate from the building itself, reaches across with a slender arch to support the wall where the thrust of the main ceiling will press it outward. (WNC.)

APSE FROM CLEVELAND PARK NEIGHBORHOOD. By the end of World War I, the rising apse at Washington National Cathedral had become a presence in the growing Cleveland Park neighborhood of northwest Washington, DC. When it was first decided to put the new cathedral on Mount St. Alban, the area was still almost rural; almost 20 years later, the city had begun to engulf the cathedral site. (WNC.)

UN-CARVED FINIALS. Later in the history of Washington National Cathedral's construction, when there was a sizeable stone-carving crew in place, there would be a dynamic between the pace of the carvers and the pace of the masons, as to whether stone would be set pre-carved or un-carved. Throughout the first decade of construction, stone would be set un-carved, like these finials on the apse buttress pinnacles. (WNC.)

THE CLOSE. Many of the ancient Gothic cathedrals in England stand on a large, walled property, referred to as a close. Washington National Cathedral's close, eventually totaling 60 acres, would be in a constant state of flux throughout the construction era, accommodating the needs of the cathedral, diocesan offices, and four schools. In 1919, there were tennis courts north of the cathedral building. (WNC.)

Three

1921–1930

STEAM SHOVELS. When the medieval Gothic cathedrals were built, the primary power source was man or animal power. By the early 1920s, construction at Washington National Cathedral had advanced to a point where multiple projects were in progress, at different locations around the building site. Steam shovels were used to excavate where the foundations of the cathedral's nave would eventually be poured. (Photograph by Commercial Photo Inc., WNC.)

PHILIP HUBERT FROHMAN AND BISHOP JAMES FREEMAN. By 1924, Washington National Cathedral would have a new architect and a new bishop. After the death of architect Henry Vaughan in 1917, and following World War I, the people building Washington National Cathedral found themselves without an architect. Having visited the cathedral in 1914, Philip Hubert Frohman (left) penned a paper suggesting a number of visual refinements to the existing plan. In 1921, Frohman was hired as the cathedral's principal architect in partnership with architects Donald Robb and Harry White. Frohman immediately referred to a coded message in the comments line of the cathedral guest log he had signed seven years earlier. It was a prayer he had left that he would be the architect of the building. Not long thereafter, Bishop Alfred Harding passed away. Harding's replacement was the Right Reverend James Edward Freeman (right). The enthusiasm and confidence Freeman brought to his office was readily evident in his expressed desire to see the cathedral completed within five years. That did not happen, but construction activities over the next decade would be driven by the energetic persistence of these two men. (WNC.)

26

POURING NAVE FOUNDATION. The foundations of Washington National Cathedral are made of unreinforced concrete. They are a minimum of 20 feet thick in all locations. Pouring foundations for the cathedral's transepts and nave covered such a large area that a system for piping concrete to all locations, from a single concrete plant and tower, had to be created. (Photograph by Commercial Photo Inc., WNC.)

BEGINNING THE CHOIR. The architectural term for the head of a Gothic great church's cruciform floor plan is choir. Washington National Cathedral's choir consists of the apse and two side-aisle chapels, north and south, to either side of the primary Great Choir center section. The side chapels would necessarily be built first. Their walls would begin rising above Bethlehem Chapel in the spring of 1922. (Photograph by Commercial Photo Inc., WNC.)

THREE MONTHS' WORK. Stonemasons, people in the stonemasonry trade, stack stone, and the way they do so has changed very little throughout the history of mankind. A crane, trowel, some mortar, a little lead, a mallet, and some rock are all the materials one needs to build an impressive and lasting edifice. The primary building stone at Washington National Cathedral is limestone from the Bedford area of southern Indiana. It weighs approximately 150 pounds per cubic foot. To avoid the rhythm of a brick pattern in the cathedral's mortar joints, the height of each course of stone and length of each block were randomized. Every block of Indiana limestone at Washington National Cathedral had a number and was custom milled for a single eventual location in the building. There was rarely more than one stone-setting crew working. (Both, photograph by Commercial Photo Inc., WNC.)

RAW LIMESTONE. At some point, deep in the earth's geologic past, land that is now southern Indiana was the bottom of a shallow ocean, containing little life larger than microscopic organisms. When those organisms died and sank to the bottom of that ocean, their remains glued the sand of the ocean bottom together. In the quarries of Bedford, Indiana, large blocks of that organically glued ocean bottom are harvested from the ground. (WNC.)

INDIANA LIMESTONE MILL. In the early building period at Washington National Cathedral, the stone was being milled by the Indiana Limestone Company of Bedford, Indiana. After large slabs of limestone were removed from the ground, they would be transported a short distance to the mill. There, the stone would be roughed into shape by large powered equipment and finished by a team of skilled stonecutters. (WNC.)

THE ENTOMBMENT OF WOODROW WILSON. Thomas Woodrow Wilson, the 28th president of the United States, died on February 3, 1924. On February 6, 1924, a private funeral conducted by Bishop James Freeman was held at the late president's private home on S Street in northwest Washington, DC. Following that service, Wilson's remains were processed up Massachusetts Avenue to Washington National Cathedral, where they would be laid to rest in the sub-crypt below Bethlehem Chapel. A cenotaph, a tomb-like memorial, would be created for him on the south side of Bethlehem Chapel. By December 28, 1956, the 100th anniversary of Wilson's birth, work on the cathedral had progressed to a point that the president's remains could be translated to a permanent tomb, in the south outer aisle of the cathedral's nave. That entire process would be overseen by a family member. (LOC.)

CRYPT CHAPEL CONSTRUCTION. In this view looking across the construction site at Washington National Cathedral in the summer of 1925, the complexity of the enterprise becomes immediately apparent. While the inner walls of the choir chapels rise, construction of the crypt level is also advancing. When architect Philip Frohman first visited the cathedral, over a decade earlier, the only worship space planned for the crypt level was Bethlehem Chapel. Crypt is an architectural term for basement, any area of a building built below ground level. Only very rarely were the crypts of ancient churches used for anything other than tombs. Bethlehem Chapel was a novelty. Frohman appreciated the idea of using the spaces of the crypt and, aware the crypts of the ancient cathedrals were often even older buildings, used each space of Washington National Cathedral's crypt to display a different architectural style precedent to that of the main level. Through the falsework of the Norman Romanesque–style Resurrection Chapel, the chevron pattern of a Norman arch is visible. As yet uncovered (lower right), interlocking Norman-style arches will embrace Resurrection Chapel's altar. (Photograph by Commercial Photo Inc., WNC.)

TOWER FOUNDATION. The foundation for Washington National Cathedral's central bell tower is massive. Huge concrete pyramids stand on top of 48 feet of unreinforced concrete, ready to receive the masonry that will become the four massive corner columns of the 301-foot, 15,000-ton tower. (Photograph by Washington Photo Service, WNC.)

RESURRECTION CHAPEL. By April 1926, the fabric of Resurrection Chapel, on the crypt level below the future site of Washington National Cathedral's south transept, was complete and ready for artistic treatment. The chapel would eventually feature a large mosaic of the resurrection of Jesus by Hildreth Meier, above the altar and mosaic panels on the walls by Rowan LeCompte. (Photograph by Washington Photo Service, WNC.)

THE COLUMNS OF ST. JOSEPH OF ARIMATHEA CHAPEL. Architect Philip Frohman felt the space between the columns of the central tower was tomb-like and chose to dedicate a chapel there to the man in whose tomb Jesus was laid to rest. The chapel would be built in the Transitional style, representing the period when England's taste in church architecture was changing from Romanesque to Gothic. (Photograph by Washington Photo Service, WNC.)

THE GEORGE A. FULLER STONE-PROCESSING PLANT. Throughout most of the construction period at Washington National Cathedral—the longest-lasting construction project in the history of Washington, DC—the George A. Fuller Company was the general contractor. By 1926, someone at that firm decided to bring the cathedral's stone milling in-house. The Fuller Company built a stone mill, just outside Washington, which would, many years later, house the Washington Episcopal School. (Photograph by Commercial Photo Co., WNC.)

THE RISING CHOIR. Whenever a new section of Washington National Cathedral was standing open, the primary elements of Gothic architecture would be plainly visible. By 1927, the choir at Washington National Cathedral had risen above the triforium level, with the chapels to either side nearing a state of as complete as can be. The open space behind the triforium arches is seen as triangular, bounded by the triforium arches, the ceiling of the chapel below, and the roof of the aisle overhead. The high arching flyers of the apse flying buttresses support the apse ceiling, while the present state of construction reveals there will be a hidden row of flyers under the triforium roof. On the crypt level, four sections of ribs stand ready for the ceiling of a north-south passageway. In the architecture of medieval Europe, the development of ribbed vaulting simplified the process of building a stone ceiling by eliminating the need to build an entire falsework for each section of stone vaulting. (Photograph by National Photo, WNC.)

St. Joseph of Arimathea Chapel. The fabric of St. Joseph of Arimathea Chapel was completed in 1927. In this chapel, the combination of ribbed vaulting, round arches in the side walls, and Norman-style embellishments on the smaller vault supporting columns captures that brief moment in English architectural history when Norman architecture was fading against the rise of the Gothic. (Photograph by Commercial Photo Co., WNC.)

Building a Crypt Aisle. As if someone knew the Great Depression were coming, vaulting over the north nave crypt aisle would be completed in less than two months. The north nave crypt aisle runs east to west below the projected north aisle of the nave, which is the long leg section of the cross-shaped floor plan. On May 14, 1929, the north nave crypt aisle was an open trench with columns. (Photograph by Commercial Photo Co., WNC.)

GROIN VAULTING. Groin vaulting is created by building intersecting round-arched tunnels, usually at right angles. The technique leaves curved ridges projecting into the enclosed space called groins. Groin vaulting is an architectural technique dating back to the early days of the Roman Empire, as is the process used to build it, falseworks. From ground level (above), the scale of the wooden structure needed to support the building of this long ceiling can be best appreciated. From a high vantage point (below), completed sections of the vaulting are visible in the foreground with the exposed falsework sections still waiting beyond. Like this one, most of the groin vaults at Washington National Cathedral are made of brick and, when completed, coated with plaster on the interior. (Both, photograph by Commercial Photo Co., WNC.)

LAWRENCE SAINT. The earliest stained glass at Washington National Cathedral, in and around Bethlehem Chapel, was created in England. The first of Washington National Cathedral's stained glass to be produced in the United States was the work of Lawrence Saint. Pictured in his studio in Huntingdon Valley, Pennsylvania, Saint (front row, with beard) instructs his staff in the proper technique for applying an opaque stain to glass. (WNC.)

NORTH NAVE CRYPT AISLE. Structurally complete by August 1929, the exposed brick of the north nave crypt aisle vault awaits a plaster finish. The length of aisle to the left would eventually be filled with a row of small, wood-constructed rooms resembling a row of monastic cells. (Photograph by Commercial Photo Co., WNC.)

THE COMPLETED CHOIR.
By the end of the 1920s
the choir at Washington
National Cathedral was
complete. The truncated
form of the building
still stood open to the
weather and offered brief
glimpses of the future,
where the built structure
waited to connect to
sections of the building.
The Great Depression
had come, and people
wondered when or even if
the cathedral would ever
be finished. (Photograph
by Underwood &
Underwood, WNC.)

BUILDING IN A GREAT DEPRESSION. By 1930, the Great Depression had deepened, almost bringing construction at Washington National Cathedral to a halt. Building at the cathedral would probably have stopped completely if not for one particular donor. James Sheldon gave several large gifts to ensure construction at the cathedral continued. Under conditions of anonymity, Sheldon stipulated that, should the cathedral need to make layoffs, higher-paid employees would go first. (Photograph by Commercial Photo Co., WNC.)

Four

1931–1940

DEPRESSION-ERA CONSTRUCTION. The generosity of James Sheldon enabled the construction of Washington National Cathedral's north transept to continue throughout the Great Depression. Sheldon's stipulation that those earning the least, to whom unemployment would be most catastrophic, be laid off last, was honored. A period when the higher-earning stone carvers were laid off but masons and laborers were not remains fixed in the cathedral's fabric. (Photograph by Commercial Photo Co., WNC.)

USING ST. JOSEPH OF ARIMATHEA CHAPEL. The completion of St. Joseph of Arimathea Chapel added a sizeable new worship space to Washington National Cathedral for the first time since the completion of Bethlehem Chapel almost 20 years earlier. While the choir and choir side chapels would open soon thereafter, St. Joseph of Arimathea Chapel was fitted with an altar rail and chairs and put into service. (WNC.)

GENERATING SUPPORT. George Wharton Pepper (left), a lifelong Episcopalian and US senator from Pennsylvania, had long thought there should be a national organization to raise funds for the building of Washington National Cathedral. Working closely with Bishop James Edward Freeman (right), Pepper helped to create the National Cathedral Association. The first president of the National Cathedral Association would be Gen. John J. "Black Jack" Pershing (center). (WNC.)

GRAND ENTRANCES. When the choir and choir side chapels of Washington National Cathedral's main level became available for use, ingress, for even the most powerful people, was through decidedly mundane construction entrances. In 1934, Bishop James Freeman (left) greeted Pres. Franklin Delano Roosevelt in what is little more than a tin shack. Accompanying the president are, from left to right, Capt. Walter Vernou, Eleanor Roosevelt, and the Roosevelts' daughter, Anna Eleanor Roosevelt Dall. (Photograph by Harris & Ewing, LOC.)

VAULTING THE CROSSING. The ceiling of the main level at Washington National Cathedral is over 100 feet above the floor. Gothic ribbed vaulting eliminates the need to construct a complete falsework for building a ceiling. Boss stones, like three-dimensional keystones, are positioned and a minimal falsework used to build the ribs. From that point on, the arching ribs provide strength and structure as the spaces between the ribs are filled. (Photograph by Commercial Photo Co., WNC.)

THE GREAT CHOIR. Although the Great Choir at Washington National Cathedral would eventually be fitted with center aisle facing, wooden choir stalls, and a large pipe organ, it was put into use as soon as wooden screens were installed to separate the Great Choir from St. Mary's Chapel in the aisle to the north and St. John's Chapel in the aisle to the south. The main altar here is called the Jerusalem Altar, and is built from stones quarried at Solomon's Quarry in Jerusalem. In the floor in front of the Jerusalem Altar are 10 stones brought from Mount Sinai in the Holy Land. The carved stone screen behind the altar contains 110 figures from the Bible and the history of Christianity, including the Right Reverend Henry Yates Satterlee, the first Episcopal bishop of Washington, DC. The role of the Cathedral Church of St. Peter and St. Paul as a cathedral for the nation is reflected in the display of state flags, projecting from the triforium. (WNC.)

Dean Noble Powell and Bishop Freeman. In 1936, the dean of Washington National Cathedral, the Very Reverend George Carl Fitch Bratenahl, suffered a stroke. Bratenahl's subsequent disability led to an unfortunate turn. Unwilling to retire or accept an emeritus position, Dean Bratenahl was forced, by the Cathedral Chapter, to retire. In 1937, Noble Cilley Powell (left), rector of Emmanuel Church in Baltimore, Maryland, was named dean of Washington National Cathedral and given the title *very reverend*. By this time, the Right Reverend James Freeman (right) had been bishop of Washington for 14 years. Powell would hold the position of dean for four years, when he would be elected Episcopal bishop of Maryland and replaced in the deanery by ZeBarney Thorne Phillips. Phillips would die suddenly, as the result of an incorrectly filled prescription, after only one year as cathedral dean. (WNC.)

THE WOMEN'S PORCH. The last major construction of the 1930s was the building of a tall porch outside Washington National Cathedral's new north transept. Two photographs from late 1937 show, with the waning of the Great Depression, work was again being accomplished at an appreciable pace. The porch of the north transept would be known as the Women's Porch and dedicated to the women of Christianity. (Both, photograph by Commercial Photo Co., WNC.)

Five

1941–1950

FOR THE DURATION. A look at Washington National Cathedral in 1941 reveals a building not half finished sitting in the midst of the evolving close. The cathedral's choir and north transept had been completed, and the south transept was beginning to rise. In the foreground is the medieval walled garden designed by Florence Bratenahl, wife of the late dean. The garden is called the Bishop's Garden. (WNC.)

QUONSET HUTS. As the United States moved to a war footing following the Japanese attack on Pearl Harbor, construction at Washington National Cathedral was halted entirely. In the meantime, the cathedral's general contractor, the George A. Fuller Company, set about building thousands of Quonset huts, which would mark the presence or passage of American military forces around the world. (LOC.)

JOINING THE WAR EFFORT. With little or no construction happening during World War II, Washington National Cathedral supported the war effort in many ways, including the creation of a salvage depot on the close, cutting up and salvaging retired or broken equipment, and holding regular prayer services for all the newcomers, military and otherwise, the war brought to Washington, DC. (Photograph by Schutz, WNC.)

EISENHOWER AND NIMITZ. In early 1946, Washington National Cathedral held a service to celebrate the end of World War II and to remember the cost. Gen. Dwight D. Eisenhower (front center, with his wife, Mamie) and Adm. Chester W. Nimitz (right, with his wife, Catherine) attended that service. Eventually, Eisenhower's funeral would be held in the cathedral. Admiral Nimitz was one of only two five-star officers in US history not to have his funeral at Washington National Cathedral. (Photograph by International News Photo, WNC.)

SOUTH TRANSEPT ENTRANCE. Following the end of World War II, Washington National Cathedral had to find its construction momentum again. By 1948, the cathedral's south transept stood looking much the same as it had seven years earlier. The completed steps, up to a functional door, allowed the unfinished portal to be used as an entrance to the main level. (Photograph by Richard Taliaferro, WNC.)

REROOFING THE NAVE CRYPT. Following completion of Washington National Cathedral's nave crypt around 1930, the exposed concrete top of the crypt, awaiting construction of the cathedral's nave, was covered and sealed with a temporary roof. By 1948, the temporary roof, nearly two decades old, had to be re-tarred. (WNC.)

SETTING A TYMPANUM. The arch-filling space above a door is called a tympanum. The tympanum over the door to the south transept is comprised of four stones surrounded by a row of smaller stones. The structural arch above the door being complete, masons then fitted the tympanum stones into the waiting space. (Photograph by Jean Speiser, WNC.)

SOUTH TRANSEPT PHASE THREE. On September 29, 1948, exactly 41 years to the day since construction at Washington National Cathedral began, a third phase of construction on the cathedral's south transept was marked by a ceremonial stone setting. As it was a Wednesday, most of the spectators were students from the National Cathedral School for Girls and St. Albans School for Boys. On the scaffolding on that day was the cathedral's new dean, the Very Reverend John W. Suter (holding trowel), with (clockwise from Suter) Head Verger James Berkeley, architect Philip Frohman, and the cathedral's business manager, Benjamin Thoron. The cathedral's master mason, Alec Ewan (back to the camera), assisted in setting the stone, along with two unidentified laborers. This third phase of south transept construction would not complete the south transept. (WNC.)

STOPPING POINTS. As the third phase of construction began on Washington National Cathedral's south transept, the work of the previous phase stands waiting as an intense jumble of exposed brick core, doorways to floors not yet built, and jagged connection points, where the new construction will interface with that built previously. (Photograph by Del Ankers, WNC.)

BISHOP DUN AND THE MASTER MASON. In 1943, at the height of World War II, Bishop James Edward Freeman passed away. Two decades had passed since Freeman had declared he would finish the cathedral in five years. Freeman was replaced by the Right Reverend Angus Dun (left), seen here receiving a masonry lesson from Master Mason Alec Ewan (right). (Photograph by Del Ankers, WNC.)

SOUTH TRANSEPT APPROACH. There is a large set of stone stairs called the Pilgrim Steps climbing the hill south of Washington National Cathedral and leading directly to the south transept entrance. Any visitor approaching the south transept from this direction in the late 1940s might have wondered whether this complex and jumbled structure would ever become a completed church. (Photograph by Del Ankers, WNC.)

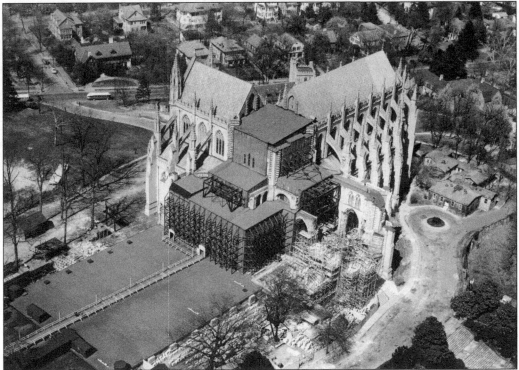

AERIAL VIEW IN 1950. In 1950, the temporary roof over the top of Washington National Cathedral's nave crypt was looking new, as was the stout temporary walling enclosing all areas of the cathedral, except the ongoing south transept construction. Beside and below the nave area (below) limestone blocks are lined up, in rank and file, awaiting their placement on the building. (Photograph by Del Ankers, WNC.)

CHRISTMAS 1951. From the completion of Bethlehem Chapel in 1912, the worship department at Washington National Cathedral fostered an ongoing tradition of large and visually elaborate Christmas pageants. The Christmas pageant of 1951 was no exception. All the figures associated with the story of the birth of Jesus are gathered on a wooden platform in the cathedral's Great Crossing, including the Star of Bethlehem, held overhead. In the background, the cathedral's choir adds music, singing from that section of the building named for that eventuality, the Great Choir. (WNC.)

Six

1951–1960

SCAFFOLDING. A hugely overlooked aspect of construction at Washington National Cathedral was the scaffolding. By 1951, most of the construction scaffolding was still made of wood, as it had been since the beginning. The scaffolding carpenters were the most overlooked group of tradesmen from the cathedral's building era, and as the cocoon of scaffolding on the south transept construction clearly shows, there were many and they were important. (WNC.)

DEAN SAYRE. Following the resignation of Dean John W. Suter in 1950, Washington National Cathedral chose a new dean in the person of the Very Reverend Francis Bowes Sayre Jr., the grandson of Pres. Woodrow Wilson. At 36 years of age, Sayre was, and remains, the youngest dean in the cathedral's history. Educated as an Episcopal priest, Sayre served as a chaplain in the US Navy during World War II, after which he served at Christ Church in Cambridge, Massachusetts, and St. Paul's Church in Cleveland, Ohio. He was seated as dean of Washington National Cathedral on May 6, 1951. Among many other accomplishments of his career, Sayre oversaw the construction of Pres. Woodrow Wilson's permanent tomb. During his administration, Sayre became committed to completing the interior of the main level by America's bicentennial. He and the cathedral builders would meet that deadline, but the financial impact of doing so would be an issue for years beyond. (WNC.)

GUASTAVINO TILE. As the north transept at Washington National Cathedral was built, and continuing into the aisles of the south transept, the cathedral builders experimented with vaulting the ceiling with an acoustic stone tile product from the Guastavino Fireproof Construction Co., instead of Indiana limestone. The vaulting process included building ribs and then a partial falsework to support setting the acoustic tile and the three layers of terra-cotta tile behind. (Photograph by Commercial Photo Co., WNC.)

BUILDING A BALCONY. At Washington National Cathedral, adding balconies to the outermost bays of the north and south transept was a modern innovation to the ancient Gothic architectural style. Very few Gothic great churches include balconies in the transepts. On July 22, 1953, stonecutter Casper Segreti (left) and Master Mason Alec Ewan (right) prepare a stone for setting in a balcony arch. (Photograph by Reni Photos, WNC.)

GARGOYLES. In architect Philip Frohman and Dean Francis Bowes Sayre Jr., Washington National Cathedral had two individuals in charge who had been introduced to the wonders of Gothic architecture as small children. The first of Washington National Cathedral's many gargoyles would adorn the west wall of the rising south transept. (Photograph by Reni Photos, WNC.)

SPIRAL STAIRS. Building the walls of Washington National Cathedral was a relatively straightforward process when compared to erecting the complexities of the south transept facade. As with all the facades surrounding the main entryways, the south transept facade would be an enormously complex building project with hidden passageways, a small elevator, and several small spiral staircases. (Photograph by Reni Photos, WNC.)

56

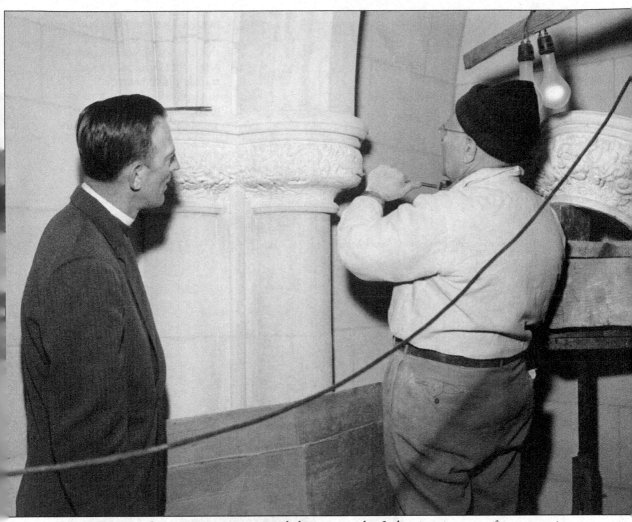

STONE CARVING. Stone carvers, a majority of whom were either Italian immigrants or first-generation Italian Americans, came and went throughout Washington National Cathedral's construction era. On becoming dean of the cathedral, Francis Bowes Sayre Jr. (left) took great interest in the work of the cathedral's artists and craftspeople, including stone carver Joseph Ratti (right). Before Ratti was employed at Washington National Cathedral, every carved feature on the building was, at least, drawn by one of the architects, from which, in most cases, a plaster model was made. Ratti did decades of this type of work, first with a studio subcontracted to produce for the cathedral and then as an employee. At some point in the late 1930s or early 1940s, Ratti convinced architect Philip Hubert Frohman that he understood the spirit of Gothic carving and felt confident he could carve certain features into the building without drawing or model. In 1955, Ratti would fall from a scaffold and become the only person to die working on construction at Washington National Cathedral. (Photograph by Del Ankers, WNC.)

SOUTH TRANSEPT BALCONY. By October 1953, work on the interior of Washington National Cathedral's south transept had advanced through completion of the south transept balcony. An arcade arch and two triforium arches, beyond and above the balcony, show how the balcony is actually fitted into the outermost bay of the transept. (Photograph by Theodore Horydczak, WNC.)

LEWIS PINS. Lifting and setting large stones involves, of course, a crane or chain-fall, but how the stone is secured to the crane is another ancient technique. Lewis pins, short stout pins of metal with a ring on the end, are inserted into two holes, angling toward one another, in the stone's upper surface. When the crane lifts by the lewis pin rings, the weight of the stone causes the pins to bind in the diagonal holes. (WNC.)

MILLIONS OF BRICKS. By the end of 1955, Frank Hagen (forward) had been a bricklayer for 50 years. Much of that time would be spent laying the brick core of Washington National Cathedral. No count was ever made of the number of bricks used in the cathedral's core, but an expert guess of several million would be reasonable. James Smith (left), foreman of the scaffolding carpenters, looks on. (Photograph by Cameramen Inc., WNC.)

MARBLE FLOORING. Most of the flooring at Washington National Cathedral is made of a variety of types and colors of marble from a variety of sources. The stone is laid out in geometric patterns designed by the cathedral's architects. The tolerances in setting the stone to the architect's plan are highly exacting, as an error of one millimeter in one location could lead to several inches of misalignment 20 yards away. (WNC.)

QUEEN ELIZABETH II AND PRESIDENT EISENHOWER. The east aisle of Washington National Cathedral's south transept is the site of War Memorial Chapel. On October 20, 1957, Queen Elizabeth II (second from left) and Prince Philip (right) visited the cathedral for the dedication of that chapel, which was a gift from the royal family, representing British gratitude for the United States' involvement in World War II. Greeted by the Right Reverend Angus Dun (third from left), the Very Reverend Francis Bowes Sayre Jr. (second from right), and Mamie and Pres. Dwight D. Eisenhower, the queen stood briefly for photographers before being led into the service by Head Verger James Berkeley (left). (WNC.)

Carl Tucker. Carl Tucker, a flutist for the Washington National Symphony, first visited Washington National Cathedral in 1957. On a subsequent visit, he had the temerity to ask a craftsman, busily and single-handedly working on the installation of the wooden enclosure around the south transept doors, whether he could help. Tucker ended up spending decades at the cathedral as an architectural modeler, wood engraver, antique clock repairer, all-around handyman, bell installer and ringer, and painter. A true polymath, Tucker would accept assignments and then teach himself the skills he needed to accomplish them. Perhaps Tucker's most visible accomplishment, the undersides of the transept balconies are both elaborately painted. Upon completion, many of the ancient Gothic cathedrals were painted, often in rich, complex patterns. Knowing this, Tucker pressed for a chance to paint something, somewhere in the cathedral. He was eventually allowed the ceilings under the transept balconies and, asked if he had ever painted before, he replied, "Of course!" and then taught himself. (Photograph by Brooks, WNC.)

SOUTH PORTAL TYMPANUM. When Bishop Angus Dun (left) and Dean Francis Bowes Sayre Jr. (right) dedicated the carving in the tympanum over the south transept door on September 20, 1959, the new sculpture was still surrounded by un-carved blanks in the archivolts overhead and the pedestal and canopy for a trumeau sculpture below. (Photograph by Bapti, WNC.)

PROCESSING FROM OUTSIDE. By the late 1950s, the processions for important services were using the center aisle of Washington National Cathedral's nave. However, Washington National Cathedral's nave had not yet been built. The center aisle was still outside and stretched across the top of the nave crypt, between rows of limestone waiting to become part of the building. (WNC.)

CATHEDRAL SCHOOL STUDENTS. Students from Washington National Cathedral's schools—the National Cathedral School for Girls, St. Albans School for Boys, and Beauvoir Elementary—were a constant presence around the cathedral's construction site. Pictured here in April 1956, National Cathedral School students, from left to right, Jan Holderness, Connie Hopkins, and Brenda Shannon stop by to watch the construction activity. (Photograph by Roland, WNC.)

THIRD PHASE OF SOUTH TRANSEPT COMPLETED. By the end of 1959, over 10 years after it had begun, the third phase of construction on Washington National Cathedral's south transept was complete. A temporary roof was placed over the otherwise open-to-the-sky south transept while the fourth phase of south transept construction was arranged. (Photograph by J.W. Stinchcomb, WNC.)

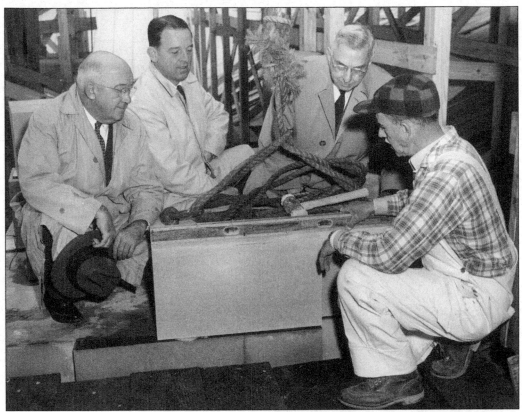

FOURTH PHASE OF SOUTH TRANSEPT CONSTRUCTION BEGINS. On April 5, 1960, with appropriate ceremony, but little fanfare, the first stone was set for phase four of Washington National Cathedral's south transept construction. Clyde Roth (left), vice president of the Fuller Construction Company, and an unidentified man watch architect Philip Frohman and Master Mason Alec Ewan place the ceremonial first stone. (Photograph by J.W. Stinchcomb, WNC.)

CARVING IN THE SOUTH TRANSEPT PORTAL. While laborers and masons build the south transept steps, scaffolding was built around the entryway's trumeau, between the doors, in preparation for carving an elaborate canopy, under which a Heinz Warneke sculpture of St. Alban will eventually be placed. (WNC.)

SOUTH TRANSEPT STONE YARD. Elaborately milled stones waiting to be craned to positions high in Washington National Cathedral's south transept stand rank and file in a stone yard located to the south of the nave crypt. Stones appearing very jagged, including the stone being lifted, are probably the most complex of the milled stones created for the cathedral. These stones are springing stones, cut for where the numerous ribs of the high vaulting gather against the wall. (Photograph by James R. Dunlop Inc., WNC.)

Seven

1961–1970

WASHINGTON NATIONAL CATHEDRAL IN THE 1960s. At Washington National Cathedral, the 1960s would bring the completion of the south transept, a massive new tower, and a significant amount of work accomplished on the cathedral's nave. As always, the complexity of the cathedral building site is bewildering, but architect Philip Frohman knew and understood every inch of it. (Photograph by Stewart Brothers, Inc., WNC.)

PINNACLES AND SCAFFOLDING. As the west clerestory of Washington National Cathedral's south transept rises above the triforium level, behind the scaffolding, so too must the external buttressing rise—eventually to a wonderland of carved stone. Everything in the stonework of Washington National Cathedral that has organic shape of form to it, in any way, is hand carved. (Photograph by Stewart Brothers, Inc., WNC.)

SOUTH TRANSEPT CLERESTORY. As with stone arches anywhere, the stones of the arches that will contain the clerestory windows of Washington National Cathedral's south transept are first set on an arch-shaped wooden frame. When the wood is removed, the downward force of gravity and the carefully angled cut of the stones hold the arch together. (Photograph by Stewart Brothers, Inc., WNC.)

BUILD THE TOWER. On May 26, 1961, the largest single construction contract to that point in the cathedral's history was signed—$1.86 million to build the central bell tower. Present at the signing are, from left to right, cathedral business manager John Bayless, Fuller Company project manager Fred J. Maynard, Fuller vice present Clyde Roth, and the Very Reverend Francis Bowes Sayre Jr. (Photograph by Brooks, WNC.)

FIRST STONE OF THE BELL TOWER. Within weeks of executing the central bell tower contract, officials of the cathedral and the general contractor gathered, again, to set the cornerstone of the cathedral's central tower. Dean Francis Bowes Sayre Jr. (front left) trowels mortar assisted by a mason, while behind, from left to right, Benjamin W. Thoron, John Bayless, Richard T. Feller, and Philip H. Frohman look on. (Photograph by Stewart Brothers, Inc.)

SOUTH TRANSEPT VAULT. As construction began on Washington National Cathedral's central tower, work continued on the fourth phase of construction on the cathedral's south transept. In September 1961, the top of the south transept's high vault was still exposed. The ribs, infill, and over-plastering provide a textbook example of a completed Gothic vault construction. (Photograph by Stewart Brothers, Inc., WNC.)

BOSSES, CARVED AND UN-CARVED. The great round keystones, where the arched ribs come together at the top of the ceiling, are called boss stones. In Washington National Cathedral's south transept, the earlier bosses went up un-carved. A technical innovation to carving brought about by Master Carver Roger Morigi and Carl Tucker allowed the later of these massive three-ton stones to be carved before installation. (Photograph by Stewart Brothers, Inc., WNC.)

SOUTH TRANSEPT ROOF.
Once the high vault in
Washington National
Cathedral's south transept
was complete, a concrete
floor was poured above,
and steel trussing (right)
was added to support the
roof. Although steel is used
in supporting the roof over
the transept, the steel is
not considered a structural
element in the cathedral,
because the building would
stand without the roof. Once
the trussing was completed,
and while work continued
on the pinnacles of the south
transept facade (below), the
roof was completed with a
standing-seam metal covering
of lead/nickel sheeting.
(Both, photograph by Stewart
Brothers, Inc., WNC.)

COMPLETING THE SOUTH TRANSEPT. On April 20, 1962, just 22 years after it was begun, Washington National Cathedral's south transept was completed by placing a stone cross on the peak of the gable end of the south transept roof. At 22 years, the south transept had taken far longer to build than any other section of the cathedral, and its completion was cause for celebration. It was also the 41st year of cathedral building for architect Philip Hubert Frohman, who had been sole architect since the passing of Donald Robb and Harry Little in the 1940s. On the scaffold, while masons and laborers align the gable cross, Frohman (right) can be seen standing with Clerk of the Works Richard T. Feller. Feller had come to the cathedral in the 1950s and taken a job as an office manager. With an education and background in civil engineering, Feller quickly advanced to the clerk of the works position, where he served as chief liaison between the cathedral and the general contractor until the cathedral building was completed. (Photograph by Stewart Brothers, Inc., WNC.)

CARVING THE SOUTH TRANSEPT BOSSES. Although the construction of Washington National Cathedral's south transept was considered complete in April 1962, carving of boss stones, which were installed blank, continued for several more months. In order to carve overhead, the carver took his measurements from a plaster model, facing him to the right. (Photograph by Stewart Brothers, Inc., WNC.)

A NEW CEILING. When the carving of the south transept bosses was completed, the platforms and scaffolding that kept the carvers close to the 100-foot ceiling were removed. For the first time in three decades, the cathedral community delighted at the sight of a brand-new section of high vaulting. (Photograph by Stewart Brothers, Inc., WNC.)

TOWER CRANE. In just two months of work, between March 28 (left) and May 29, 1962, (below), the lower bell chamber in Washington National Cathedral's central tower doubled in height—a breakneck pace by cathedral standards. Above it all, and speeding the work significantly, stands one of this cathedral's builders' greatest claims to fame. On a trip to Canada, Philip Hubert Frohman saw a revolutionary new crane. It was a luffing-jib balance crane with an enormous reach, operating from a single tower. The crane was a product of the Linden Company in Sweden. As soon as he saw it, Philip Frohman knew this was exactly what he needed for building the cathedral's central tower. When purchased by and brought to Washington National Cathedral, the Linden crane pictured was the first such tower crane to be used in the United States. (Both, photograph by Stewart Brothers, Inc., WNC.)

BISHOP CREIGHTON. In 1962, Rev. William Forman Creighton was elected to succeed the retiring Angus Dun as Episcopal bishop of Washington. His first major moment as leader of a community building a great church was the ground breaking for the first of two low wings, south and north, architect Philip Frohman added to the plan for the cathedral's west tower complex. The southern wing would house the Rare Book Library. (Photograph by Stewart Brothers, Inc., WNC.)

RARE BOOK LIBRARY EXCAVATION. Excavation for Frohman's two low wings was complicated by the need to work around deep concrete foundations poured over four decades earlier. (Photograph by Stewart Brothers, Inc., WNC.)

THE KIBBEY CARILLON. The Kibbey Carillon, a 53-bell instrument given to Washington National Cathedral by Bessie J. Kibbey, was cast at the John Taylor Bell Foundry in Loughboro, England (left). The John Taylor Bell Foundry occupies a curious but important niche in the history of the United States. The Taylor Foundry cast America's Liberty Bell. While visiting the foundry, the cathedral's clerk of the works, Richard Feller, jokingly suggested faulty workmanship to the case of the Liberty Bell's famous crack. A quick-witted Taylor executive quickly replied, "We told you Yanks, years ago. Just return the bell to us, in its original packaging, and we'll take care of it." The smallest and largest of the Kibbey Carillon bells (below) weigh 17 pounds and 12 tons, respectively. (Left, photograph by Barratt's Photo Press Ltd., WNC; below, photograph by P.A. Reuter Ltd., WNC.)

ARRIVAL AND INSTALLATION OF THE CARILLON. The day the Kibbey Carillon arrived at Washington National Cathedral (above) was an exciting one, as a long line of trucks pulled up the north driveway, carrying the voice of one incredibly massive musical instrument. Over the following few weeks (right), the bells would be lifted, one by one, to a large platform above. That platform was built at the level of the peak of the north transept roof, and stretched east, like a runway, from above the lift staging area to the peak of the north transept roof. There, the runway turned south and traveled along the roof ridge to the side of the central tower, where a large opening had been left in the side wall of the bell chamber. (Both, WNC.)

HIGH ABOVE WASHINGTON. By late September 1963, just 2.5 years after it was started, Washington National Cathedral's bell tower was almost complete. It did not take workers long to realize that the view of Washington, DC, from the top of the tower, was unsurpassed. At 301 feet above grade, Washington National Cathedral's central tower is not the tallest building in Washington. The Washington Monument is over 250 feet taller. However, Washington National Cathedral is sitting on land much higher than the Washington Monument, and, at 676 feet above sea level, the cathedral's tower is the highest point in the city. (Photograph by Stewart Brothers, Inc., WNC.)

ONE BIG, HAPPY FAMILY. The day the final stone of the tower was to be set, architect Philip Frohman gathered with key figures in the tower's construction for a group photograph. In a moment of levity, Frohman threatened to smash a carved finial. Besides Frohman (to the right of the finial, wielding a mallet), the group includes Master Carver Roger Morigi (to the left of the finial, reaching toward Frohman), sculptor/carvers Constantine Seferlis (third row, left) and John Guarente (second row, third from left), carver Gino Bresciani (first row, left), modeler Carl Bush (second row, left), and Clerk of the Works Richard Feller (far right), among others. (Photograph by Stewart Brothers, Inc., WNC.)

GLORIA IN EXCELSIS. On October 29, 1963, Washington National Cathedral's central bell tower was completed. In addition to the Kibbey Carillon, the tower houses the heaviest 10-bell set of peal bells in North America. On its dedication the following spring, the tower was officially named the Gloria in Excelsis (Glory to God in the highest) Tower. (Photograph by Stewart Brothers, Inc., WNC.)

TOWER TOAST. Following the ceremonial setting of the stone completing Washington National Cathedral's central tower, cathedral officials and the construction crew gathered on the roof of the tower to celebrate. All the most visible of the cathedral's community were there. In this moment of triumph, the dean, architect, master carver, and clerk of the works celebrated shoulder-to-shoulder with the masons, carvers, bricklayers, crane operators, and, most important of all, the many unheralded laborers who mixed mortar and lifted and lugged throughout the entire process. The celebration included a champagne toast. While the little paper cups were inexpensive, it is most certain the champagne was not. (Photograph by Stewart Brothers, Inc., WNC.)

RARE BOOK LIBRARY CONSTRUCTION IN WINTER. Work continued on Washington National Cathedral's Rare Book Library, architect Philip Frohman's low southern addition to the west tower block, through the end of 1963 and into 1964. Throughout that winter, the scaffolding around the worksite was wrapped in plastic sheeting (above) to keep the weather outside, as much as possible. There are temperatures below which mortar is compromised and stone or brick should not be set. Nonetheless, by March 1964, the bosses and ribs of the Rare Book Library's vaulted ceiling were in place (below) and ready to have stone infill set between them. (Both, photograph by Stewart Brothers, Inc., WNC.)

SOUTH NAVE OUTER AISLE. In the logical order of constructing Washington National Cathedral's 100-foot-tall nave, the lowest outermost portions of the room were built first. The nave would have five aisles, the outermost of which would run west to east through the bases of the nave buttresses. Philip Frohman designed this aisle in an effort to move the individualities of memorial architecture one step further from the center aisle. For years, these outer nave aisles would sit out ahead of the rest of the nave construction, like the two front legs of a sphinx. From outside (above), the outer aisle is seen to reach all the way to the Rare Book Library and features a row of un-carved gargoyles. Seen from the center aisle (below), the open expanse, where the aisle will eventually connect to the room, is covered with temporary walls. (Both, photograph by Stewart Brothers, Inc., WNC.)

NAVE CONSTRUCTION OVERVIEW. Seen from above in a view looking west in late July 1965, the area of Washington National Cathedral's unbuilt nave is so expansive, it is like a village unto itself. The north outer aisle is being constructed, under wraps, to the right, as is a main arcade column. Other columns, built and temporarily roofed, are also visible, with a complex of offices and work spaces sprawling beyond. (Photograph by Stewart Brothers, Inc., WNC.)

KIRKIN O' THE TARTAN. The Kirkin o' the Tartan, a service blessing the Scottish clans in America, came to Washington National Cathedral in the late 1950s and was the author's introduction to the cathedral, when he was a toddler. In 1966, the author's father, John E. Bittner, played the tenor drum for the Washington Bagpipe Band. Stories about processing through the construction entrance, playing a drum, and coming into the cavernous interior, were told at the Bittner dinner table for decades. (Photograph by Jane Bittner.)

BUILDING THE NORTH NAVE TRIFORIUM. During the week between Christmas 1967 and New Year's Day 1968, masons continued to work on the north triforium of Washington National Cathedral's nave. Holland Survis (right) shared the work with a fellow mason identified only as Reginald. (Photograph by Stewart Brothers, Inc., WNC.)

BUILDING THE SOUTH NAVE CLERESTORY. As construction on the cathedral's nave clerestory progressed through September 1968, it was plain to see just how little mass there is to a Gothic clerestory. The taller nearer stone pylons are the only structural solid to the clerestory. The large voids in between will contain windows and fine stone tracery. The gabled structures, beyond, are the nave buttresses rising outside the wall. (Photograph by Stewart Brothers, Inc., WNC.)

84

ROWAN LECOMPTE. Rowan LeCompte first visited Washington National Cathedral at the age of 14. Intrigued by the stained glass, he taught himself from a public library book on stained glass and had his first window in the cathedral at the age of 16. Among many others, he designed all 18 of Washington National Cathedral's nave clerestory windows and the Creation Rose window above the center west portal. (Photograph by Don Callander, WNC.)

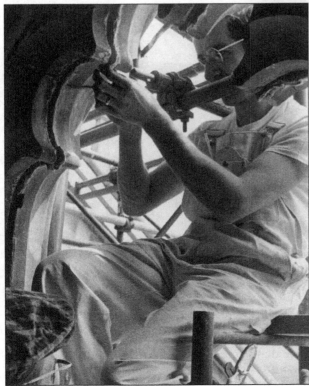

DIETER GOLDKUHLE. The Goldkuhle family of Weidenbruck, Germany, was already steeped in the glass trades when Dieter Goldkuhle was born in 1938. After years of stained-glass apprenticeship in Europe, Goldkuhle emigrated to the United States in 1962 and began working on Washington National Cathedral's glass in 1966. Goldkuhle became an innovator in the stained-glass-fabrication field and continued to work on the cathedral's glass until his death in 2011. (WNC.)

PLACING NAVE BOSSES. Each of the main bosses for the center rib of Washington National Cathedral's nave vaulting weighs over three tons and was carved before being raised to the height of the center rib. The process used to move these stones down the length of the center rib line probably dates back to that point in human history when humans started working with stone and realized round things roll. The boss stone, art down, is raised on four stone stumps, left during the

carving process. The four stumps then sit on a thick disc of plywood, which, in turn, is sitting on two relatively short lengths of wooden two-by-six supports. That assembly is then moved down two long sets of four-by-four wooden rails running the length of the center rib line, propelled by an iron pry bar and rolling over four rounded logs. (Photograph by Morton Broffman.)

DAVE BRUBECK. Washington National Cathedral enjoyed a long relationship with legendary jazz pianist Dave Brubeck. In February 1969, Brubeck recorded his oratorio *The Light in the Wilderness* for television broadcast. The performance was broadcast on CBS on the evening of April 4, 1969. (WNC.)

NAVE VAULTING CONSTRUCTION. By late summer 1969, the structure of Washington National Cathedral's nave ceiling was beginning to take shape. After placing the main bosses on the center line of the nave and the secondary bosses around them, the process of connecting them with ribs began. (Photograph by Stewart Brothers, Inc., WNC.)

RIBBED VAULTING INFILL. Once a section of Washington National Cathedral's vault ribbing was completed, the infilling process began. Set row upon row, each row supporting the next, wider and wider tiers of infill stones span the gaps between the vault ribs until the ceiling appears solid behind the ribs. (Photograph by Stewart Brothers, Inc., WNC.)

PREPARING TO TOP A VAULT. By March 31, 1970, a large section of the nave vaulting at Washington National Cathedral was ready to be topped. Walls were built on the main transverse ribs, which sit perpendicular to the center rib. Those walls were then raised to a uniform height, the same as that of the outer walls. This process provided a level surface on which to build the cathedral's nave overcroft floor. (Photograph by Stewart Brothers, Inc., WNC.)

FIRST STONE OF THE WEST TOWERS. Although a more formal cornerstone would be set later in the year, Project Manager Fred Maynard (far left), Clerk of the Works Richard Feller (second row, in shirt and tie), and architect Philip Hubert Frohman (far right) joined masons and laborers for the setting of the first stone of Washington National Cathedral's St. Paul Tower, the first of the two towers of the cathedral's west front. (Photograph by Stewart Brothers, Inc., WNC.)

ROOFING THE NAVE. Summer 1970 saw the building of a large section of nave roof above the newly completely areas of vaulting. The roof, built before pouring the floor of the overcroft, would provide protection from the elements while the construction of the overcroft continued. (Photograph by Stewart Brothers, Inc., WNC.)

Eight
1971–1980

THE CHRISTMAS CRANE. The presence of the Linden crane on the Washington National Cathedral building site allowed for the development of a Christmastime lighting tradition. Each year, as the Christmas season approached, cathedral staff would decorate the crane with a cross of lights. (Photograph by Stewart Brothers, Inc., WNC.)

WAITING FOR CONNECTION. By 1971, with Washington National Cathedral's west towers under construction, work on the cathedral's nave slowed. The towers and narthex between constitute the west end of the nave, so the nave waited for connection to the rising tower. (Photograph by H. Byron Chambers, WNC.)

ARCHES AND TRACERY. The interior spaces at the bottom of each of Washington National Cathedral's west towers are called porches. When finished, daylight will pour in through the gated portals and on into the nave by way of beautiful arches filled with white-glass (clear) over the nave doors. In March 1971, workers build one such arch; the arch to the left has also had the tracery installed. (Photograph by Stewart Brothers, Inc., WNC.)

Southwest Tower Portal. As the west towers at Washington National Cathedral rose in spring 1971, the arched form of the cathedral's main entrances took shape, each with a broad expanse of stone above the door that would eventually be elaborately carved. (Photograph by Stewart Brothers, Inc., WNC.)

Inside a Tower Porch. The tower porches at Washington National Cathedral would eventually become grand, bright open spaces. However, as they were built, crowded by scaffolding, inside and out, the interior spaces became crowded dark work spaces. (Photograph by Stewart Brothers, Inc., WNC.)

FROHMAN SETS TOWER CORNERSTONE. Because the official name of Washington National Cathedral is the Cathedral Church of St. Peter and St. Paul, the two west towers, north and south, are named St. Peter and St. Paul, respectively. On September 29, 1971, the 64th anniversary of the setting of the cathedral's foundation stone and the 50th year since Philip Hubert Frohman had become the cathedral's principal architect, the 84-year-old Frohman troweled mortar for the setting of the St. Peter tower cornerstone. Frohman would continue to climb the cathedral's scaffolding almost every day until he was hit by a car on the cathedral's driveway in August of the following year. Frohman would pass away just over two months later, on October 30, 1972. Along with a deeply bereaved family and cathedral community, he left behind a completed plan for his beloved cathedral. (WNC.)

WINTERIZED. Covering a worksite like Washington National Cathedral's growing west towers for winter was a complex task in itself. As 1971 turned to 1972, the southwest tower, St. Paul, was covered in a bewildering array of small shedding roofs, all to keep weather away from the ongoing work. By this time, the press was on for finishing the nave by the US bicentennial. (Photograph by Stewart Brothers, Inc., WNC.)

RIB CONSTRUCTION FRAMING. Small inner recesses within Washington National Cathedral's larger west tower porches, called exedras, involved tight complex rib structures in their vaulted ceilings. Often, the frameworks used to construct these critical arches were prefabricated and tested in a cathedral work shed. (Photograph by Stewart Brothers, Inc., WNC.)

BOSSES FOR AN EXEDRA VAULT. The time-tested technique of bosses first, followed by ribbing, is used on ceilings of every scale. Vaulting an exedra ceiling in March 1972, the bosses stand and wait, as a mason (lower right) begins to build ribs that will reach upward to meet them. (Photograph by Stewart Brothers, Inc.)

FILLING AN EXEDRA VAULT. Lengths of infill stone are custom cut and hand set, beginning at the bottom, in the gaps between the ribs. The fit is so tight, the ribs pick up most of the weight of the infill and carry it into the columns below. (Photograph by Stewart Brothers, Inc., WNC.)

CENTER AISLE INTO THE CAVERNOUS NAVE. The primary center portal in Washington National Cathedral's west facade is built to be the main entrance to the main level. When completed, a visitor entering will walk up a set of stairs, between two sets of three empty statuary niches, left and right, and into a center-aisle porch, known as a narthex. From there, one more set of doors will lead into the nave. In 1972, as this primary portal was rising past the empty statuary niches, the cavern of the massive nave waited beyond with its inconspicuous construction entrance hiding amidst the scaffolding. (Photograph by Norman McGrath, WNC.)

CENTER TYMPANUM. As 1972 came to a close, stone for a massive relief sculpture had been placed above the door of Washington National Cathedral's impending main entrance. The sculpture image, *Ex Nihilo*, would be created by a stone-carving apprentice from the cathedral's workshop, Frederick Hart. Hart's first job at the cathedral was as a mailroom clerk. By the end of his sculptural career, he would become, perhaps, the Michelangelo of the 20th century. (Photograph by Stewart Brothers, Inc., WNC.)

WEST BALCONY. Despite the death of architect Philip Frohman in the fall of the previous year, spring 1973 saw the product of his genius continuing to rise. Inspired by the innovative balconies in Washington National Cathedral's north and south transepts, Frohman carried the concept to the west end of the building, placing a balcony at the west end of the nave between the towers and over the narthex. (Photograph by Stewart Brothers, Inc., WNC.)

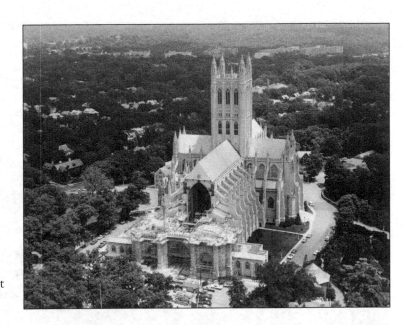

NAVE'S WESTERN INTERIOR ELEVATION. The design Philip Hubert Frohman provided for the west wall of Washington National Cathedral's nave, above the balcony, may be among his greatest achievements. While the nave's western terminus would eventually be dominated by the elaborate Creation Rose window with its incredible Rowan LeCompte glass, the three tall, slender columns below add a tremendous vertical emphasis to the room. (Photograph by Stewart Brothers, Inc., WNC.)

ROOM FOR STATUARY. Nine empty statuary niches above the main center portal at Washington National Cathedral appear relatively small from the ground. However, the sight of a mason setting the stones for those niches gives scale to spaces that may, someday, accommodate larger-than-life statues. (Photograph by Stewart Brothers, Inc., WNC.)

SETTING THE WEST NAVE CLERESTORY. In 1974, as Washington National Cathedral's west towers approached the height of connection to the upper nave, work on the westernmost bays of the nave continued through the clerestory window level. Seen here, masons and laborers gather around the top of one window, ready to manhandle one large section of the window arch into place. (Photograph by Stewart Brother, Inc., WNC.)

PRESENTING THE MOON. On July 21, 1974, the five-year anniversary of man's first steps on the moon, the crew of NASA's Apollo 11 mission, Edwin "Buzz" Aldrin (left), Neil Armstrong (center), and Michael Collins came to Washington National Cathedral. The astronauts brought with them a piece of moon rock they had collected on their mission and presented it across the cathedral's Jerusalem Altar to the Very Reverend Francis Bowes Sayre Jr., who is seen holding the precious stone aloft. It is the tendency of Washington National Cathedral's elder siblings, the ancient cathedrals of Europe, to serve, among many other ways, as time capsules for the people who built them. To be mounted in a beautiful window, honoring those in the fields of science and technology, perhaps this small piece of the moon will become the great secular relic of 20th-century mankind. (WNC.)

WEST TOWER INTERIOR. To a level over 100 feet above the ground, Washington National Cathedral's west towers and the west end of the nave, inside, are integrated into one large block of structure. The top of this block will include one spacious level, an observation gallery, of the same footprint as the porches and narthex below. In each tower, between the porches and the observation gallery, are six levels of stairs, offices, and other facilities. (Photograph by Stewart Brothers, Inc., WNC.)

BOTTOM OF A ROSE. By late summer 1974, the west balcony and the wall above it were complete, and work had moved on to the setting of the west rose window. With only the bottom arc in place, the proportions of the enormous circular window are already easily understood. (Photograph by Stewart Brothers, Inc., WNC.)

STONE SPOKES ON A WHEEL. Designing and setting the tracery of a great rose window is one of the great engineering accomplishments of Gothic architecture. Tons of stone block will eventually appear as light and delicate as a spider's web, but getting all of the stone in place and supporting itself is a mighty accomplishment. (Photograph by Stewart Brothers, Inc., WNC.)

NARTHEX FLOOR. The floor of Washington National Cathedral's narthex, the entryway behind the center portal doors, includes 52 circular marble seals decorated with the seals of the 50 states, the District of Columbia, and the nation. This stonemason is setting the seal of the State of Arkansas. (Photograph by Morton Broffman, WNC.)

TOP OF THE WEST ROSE. More than one year after beginning work on Washington National Cathedral's west rose window, masons and laborers set the stones that will be the top of the circular window. While the tracery of the entire window was yet to be finished, topping out the structure was a noteworthy moment. (Photograph by Stewart Brothers, Inc., WNC.)

WEST BALCONY BOSSES. When architect Philip Frohman passed away in 1972, his plan specified a ribbed barrel vault for the ceiling over Washington National Cathedral's west balcony. Afterward, it was decided the space would be better ceilinged with a Gothic ribbed vault that matched the rest of the room, but 11 new bosses and half-bosses in the west end of the room presented an iconographic problem, until Richard Feller mentioned Moses and the 10 Commandments. (Photograph by Stewart Brothers, Inc., WNC.)

REMARKABLE VIEWS. Workers high on Washington National Cathedral's construction always had the opportunity and the distraction risk of panoramic views from above any other point in the nation's capital. Almost 30 miles to the north, Sugarloaf Mountain was plainly visible, as were the Blue Ridge Mountains 60 miles to the west, but any glance to the south was over the confluence of the Potomac and Anacostia Rivers, where the nation's monuments and governmental buildings stood gleaming in the sun. In this 1975 view, through the top of a clerestory window in the cathedral's southwest nave, the sights include the Washington Monument, and one scaffolding box to the right, the Jefferson Memorial and a rare glimpse of the US Naval Observatory, which would become the official residence of the vice president of the United States during the administration of Pres. Ronald Reagan. (Photograph by Stewart Brothers, Inc., WNC.)

ISIDORO FLAIM. Stonemason Isidoro Flaim would work at Washington National Cathedral for over 30 years. Here, early on, Flaim checks the alignment of a wooden frame that will have to support the ribs of the cathedral's west balcony ceiling. (Photograph by Stewart Brothers, Inc., WNC.)

NAVE MEETING WEST NAVE FACADE. Blind tracery is created by applying tracery forms to a solid wall. With no window or openings through the tracery, the effect is purely decorative. The blind tracery decorations above the west rose window bring that plane of the cathedral's west facade to within a few feet of where it will meet the ceiling above the nave's west balcony. (WNC.)

ULRICH HENN. On completion, the portals of Washington National Cathedral's west facade would be adorned and secured by six pairs of enormous cast-bronze gates that were the work of German sculptor Ulrich Henn (right). It took Henn 12 years to sculpt the one-to-one-scale wax panels that would be used for forming the bronze in the lost-wax process of metal casting. (WNC.)

STONE YARD. By the mid-1970s, the stones that would be used to complete Washington National Cathedral's nave were being lined up, rank and file, each one with a number and eventual location, in the oak grove to the west of the cathedral. Each stone placed required a laborer or mason's assistant to go to the front yard with a cart and chain fall to bring the stone to its building location. (Photograph by Stewart Brothers, Inc., WNC.)

THE NAVE FLOOR. As the rush to complete Washington National Cathedral's nave by America's bicentennial intensified, teams of stone-flooring experts cut a variety of types of marble to complete the complex pattern of the cathedral's main floor. Measured thrice and cut once, the stones were then set on a full bed of grout and adjusted to incredibly detailed specifications that had been provided by Philip Frohman before his death. There are some who work in the trade that have declared Washington National Cathedral's flooring a wonder of the world in that everything lines up neatly over nearly 80,000 square feet of floor. (Both, photograph by Stewart Brothers, Inc., WNC.)

THE NAVE. Spring 1976 saw the fulfillment of Dean Francis Bowes Sayre Jr.'s wishes, with the fabric of Washington National Cathedral's nave completed and ready for dedication. The installation of the nave's stained glass and the carving of stone features around the room would continue for more than 25 more years, but the nation's 200th birthday was fast approaching, and thanks to Dean Sayre's vision, the cathedral's nave could be dedicated and presented to the nation as a huge birthday gift. The guest list for this particular party was impressive. (Photograph by Stewart Brothers, Inc., WNC.)

RETURN OF THE QUEEN. On July 8, 1976, Queen Elizabeth II of Great Britain returned to Washington National Cathedral to witness and take part in the dedication of the cathedral's nave. The queen dedicated a stone version of the cathedral's official seal, which had been set into the floor at the west end of the center aisle. After the service, Queen Elizabeth was accompanied by Canon Sanford Garner (left) and Head Verger John Kraus (right). The front line of luminaries seeing her off (below) was worthy of the occasion and includes, from left to right in the first row, Dean Sayre, Pres. Gerald R. Ford, Bishop William F. Creighton, Canon John T. Walker, and First Lady Betty Ford. Within two years, Canon Walker would succeed Creighton as bishop of Washington and Sayre as dean of the cathedral, uniting the two positions for the first time since Bishop Harding appointed Dean Bratenahl in 1916. (Both, photograph by Morton Broffman, WNC.)

A "New" Stone Mill. Doing what it took to complete Washington National Cathedral's nave by 1976, Dean Francis B. Sayre Jr. and other cathedral decisionmakers put the cathedral in a precarious financial situation. At the time, the situation was such that people were wondering how much longer work could continue and whether Sayre's rush had jeopardized the whole project. The George Fuller Construction Company had closed its stone mill in nearby Maryland at the beginning of World War II, and since then all the cathedral stone milling reverted to the mill in Indiana. In 1977, in an effort to reduce the cost of construction, the cathedral purchased an existing stone mill (above) in northeast Washington. Not long thereafter, the cathedral's own mill began receiving and milling large blocks of Indiana limestone (right). (Above, WNC; right, photograph by Morton Broffman.)

DIETER GOLDKUHLE INSTALLING MOON ROCK. Sometimes it can take time to get things done at Washington National Cathedral, and even more so during the construction era. The Scientists and Technicians window, by artist Rodney Winfield, now more popularly known as the Space window, was in its place and dedicated on the same day the Apollo 11 crew presented the moon rock in 1974. It would be almost three years before the lunar sample would be installed in Winfield's beautiful window. The cathedral's moon rock is a disc-shaped rock sample that weighs 7.18 grams. Although the stone is mostly composed of basalt, it also contained a mineral, pyroxferroite, previously unknown on earth. The sample was carefully placed in an airtight nitrogen-filled disc and, on March 29, 1977, was installed in the Space window by the cathedral's meticulous glass fabricator, Dieter Goldkuhle. (WNC.)

ROGER MORIGI. Born in Italy, Roger Morigi would serve as Washington National Cathedral's master carver for over 25 years. On his path to that career, he also carved, among many other works, the statuary over the entrance to the US Supreme Court in Washington, DC, and the *Nittany Lion* in Penn State University's Lion Shrine. At the cathedral, among many other works, Morigi carved *Jesus* behind the Jerusalem Altar, and Heinz Warneke's *Last Supper* in the south transept portal. (WNC.)

INSTALLING ADAM. The theme chosen for art adorning the west portals at Washington National Cathedral was creation. Frederick Hart's sculptures of the creation of day, night, and mankind would eventually fill the portal tympanums. Roger Morigi's last great carving would be of Hart's sculpture of Adam. Seen here, Morigi (white hat) directs Frank Zic (lower left), Vincent Palumbo (upper right with white gloves), and others in placing the *Adam* statue between the main center doors. (WNC.)

WORK STOPPAGE. By 1978, Washington National Cathedral's increasingly dire financial circumstances finally brought work to a stop. Cathedral family and outside observers alike wondered aloud whether the cathedral would ever be finished. The Pilgrim Observation Gallery, the level at the top of the west tower block, stood partially vaulted and open to the sky for almost two years. (Photograph by Stewart Brothers, Inc., WNC.)

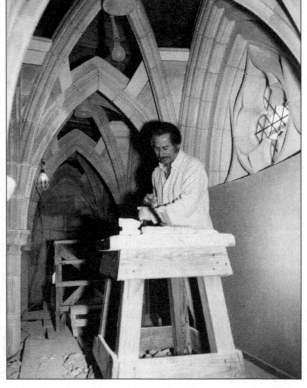

WORK RESUMES. In 1980, workers who had been laid off but were happy to return to cathedral work included stonecutter and mason Carlo Donofrio, who picked up where work had left off in 1978, cutting and fitting infill for the Pilgrim Observation Gallery vault. (Photograph by Stewart Brothers, Inc., WNC.)

Nine

1981–1990

Two Towers. In the 1980s, the two west towers at Washington National Cathedral would rise independently but simultaneously above the Pilgrim Observation Gallery. On the exterior, each architectural level, as it rose above the last, would be richly adorned with gargoyles, carved animals, caricatures of the carvers, musical instrument–playing angels, and, as the result of a schoolchildren's competition, a carving of Darth Vader. (Photograph by Lautman, WNC.)

PILGRIM OBSERVATION GALLERY. The Pilgrim Observation Gallery, at the top of Washington National Cathedral's west tower block, was finished by April 1982. When it was opened to the public later that year, visitors finally got to see what cathedral workers had been seeing for decades, the finest views of the Washington, DC, area anywhere. Offering a nearly 360-degree view of the surrounding area, the Pilgrim Observation Gallery also connects to an auditorium that sits beneath the west end of the nave roof. In the few degrees where the long view is obscured, incredible views of the high exterior of the nave, including the nave's flying buttresses, are offered. (Photograph by Stewart Brothers, Inc., WNC.)

CONSTRUCTION SHEDS.
As the main entrances
at Washington National
Cathedral were completed,
work yards and construction
sheds that had stood for
decades and contained
entire careers would need to
be removed. The cathedral
construction site had always
been dotted with temporary
work structures. They rose,
moved, and were torn down,
but there were some that
had been around as long as
anyone alive could remember.
(Photograph by Stewart
Brothers, Inc., WNC.)

GRADING THE FRONT COURT. Once the old construction site work sheds were removed, Washington National Cathedral's front courtyard was graded and paved with granite Belgian block. The courtyard was named Walker Court, in memory of the Right Reverend John T. Walker, Bishop of Washington, who would pass away, suddenly, on September 29, 1989, the 82nd anniversary of the cathedral's foundation stone and one year short of the cathedral's completion. (Photograph by Stewart Brothers, Inc., WNC.)

BILLY CLELAND. Peter Cleland, with both his father and grandfather named William Cleland, was never called Peter. On the Washington National Cathedral construction site, where he served as master mason from 1971 until his retirement in 1989, he was always known as "Billy." Cleland had briefly served the cathedral earlier in his career, and, in the meanwhile, among other jobs, set the stones for the grave of Pres. John F. Kennedy. (WNC.)

THE FINAL CREW. Rarely during the building of the cathedral did the number of the working crew exceed 40; during the final decade, it never exceeded 30. The entire crew gathered for this photograph during the final years of construction. Pictured are, from left to right, (first row) J.C. Thomas (laborer), Andrew Uhl (stone carver), Dale Smith (laborer), Joseph Alonso (mason foreman), and Patrick Plunkett (stone carver); (second row) Otto Epps (laborer), William "Billy" Cleland Jr. (apprentice mason), Richard Bird (crane operator), Sterling Proctor (laborer), and Jacob Pinckney (laborer); (third row) Matthew Girard (stone carver), David Roberts (stone carver), Kurt Kiefer (stone carver), Ray Cleland (laborer), Peter "Billy" Cleland (master mason), and Mike O'Connor (carpenter); (fourth row) Isidoro Flaim (stonemason), William Bucher (stone carver), Wayne Ferree (stone carver), Edward Jackson (laborer), Sean Calahan (stone carver), Vincent Palumbo (master carver), and Brian Murphy (stone carver). (WNC.)

ELECTRICITY. One modernism always present at Washington National Cathedral was electricity, and electricians were always an important part of cathedral operations. Greg Addison (left), working with Richard Pence, first worked on the cathedral's grounds crew in 1979. He became a cathedral electrician and, as of the writing of this book, has served in that position for 28 years. (Photograph by Morton Broffman.)

A CONSTANT TASK. Indiana limestone, a porous stone, contains a dark brown and black impurity, which leeches to the surface as a wet stone dries. When a roof leaks, the water falls on top of and then permeates through stone ceilings, leaving an unsightly stain. Cathedral mason Isidoro Flaim applies a poultice that, when dried and removed, will take the stain with it. (Photograph by Morton Broffman.)

RESTORING BEFORE COMPLETION. Masonry maintenance is a constant at super-massive masonry structures like Washington National Cathedral. Time, weather, shifting, and settling constantly work the stone and the mortar between. Repairing mortar, a process called tuck-pointing, is a near constant. In the years just before the cathedral's completion, a massive tuck-pointing operation made uniform the mortar from many different vault construction periods. The scaffolding for this project (left) was a wonder itself, and the process for moving it down the length of the nave on runners seemed entirely ancient at the same time. (Both, photograph by Morton Broffman.)

ABOVE THE TOWER ROOFS. A look at Washington National Cathedral on March 29, 1989 (right), shows completion of the St. Peter (left) and St. Paul (right) towers to the roof level and work proceeding on the pinnacles that will rise above. When completed, the main pinnacles will appear to be eight spikes, one on each of the four corners of each of the towers, but the actual size of small features on the massive building can be deceiving. The pinnacles of the west towers at Washington National Cathedral will themselves be, when completed, four-story-tall towers. A closer look at a workman on the walkway between the two towers (below) lends perspective. (Both, photograph by John W. Wrigley, WNC.)

JOE ALONSO. Joseph Alonso joined the masonry crew building Washington National Cathedral in 1985. By 1989, he was working as mason foreman under the direction of Master Mason Peter "Billy" Cleland. When Cleland retired, the cathedral retired the master mason title with him. Alonso became a major figure in the construction and ongoing life of Washington National Cathedral, sometimes even finding himself in a spokesman role. He is, perhaps, the last of the great cathedral builders, but that story has not ended yet. As of the writing of this book, 30 years after coming to the cathedral, Alonso continues to serve as the cathedral's mason foreman. (Photograph by Morton Broffman.)

REACHING THE TOP. By July 1989, the pinnacles on top of Washington National Cathedral's west towers neared completion (above). The final stone of the northwest tower would be placed before the end of the year. Time was growing short for the cathedral builders to savor this experience of a lifetime. Below, three members of Washington National Cathedral's final construction crew—from left to right, J.C. Thomas, Isidoro Flaim, and Raymond Cleland—gather around a pinnacle on the cathedral's southwest tower, with carved angels and crockets all about. (Both, photograph by Stewart Brothers, Inc., WNC.)

HEART OF THE NEIGHBORHOOD. In just over nine decades, since the purchase of the Mount St. Alban property, the land around Washington National Cathedral went from nearly rural, to suburban, to an affluent urban residential area, and the cathedral went from being a new neighbor in a new neighborhood to being the heart of a whole section of the city. The cathedral's bells could be heard many city blocks away, and the cathedral's towers could be seen from vantage points around the city. (Photograph by John W. Wrigley, WNC.)

PRESIDENTIAL MATTERS. September 29, 1990, the 83rd anniversary of the setting of Washington National Cathedral's foundation stone, was the day Washington National Cathedral would be completed, and the milestone was widely heralded. Close to 25,000 people gathered to watch the setting of the final stone, and shortly before midday, a presidential limousine arrived, bringing Pres. George H.W. Bush to speak at the ceremony. (Photograph by Susan Jensen.)

THE FINAL FINIAL. The final stone placed on Washington National Cathedral, completing the 83-year construction process, was a 1,008-pound piece of Indiana limestone, carved into the flower-like shape of a Gothic finial. Ceremonially sent from the ground by retiring Master Mason Billy Cleland, it was, on reaching the top, guided into place by Mason Foreman Joseph Alonso. Also present on the pinnacle scaffolding that day were cathedral laborer Otto Epps and Clerk of the Works Richard T. Feller. (Photograph by Susan Jensen.)

COMPLETION. Just past noon on September 29, 1990, waves of cheering and applause from thousands of enthusiastic onlookers climbed Washington National Cathedral's southwest tower to where laborer Otto Epps (partially hidden, left), Mason Foreman Joe Alonso (center), and Clerk of the Works Richard T. Feller had just completed the construction of Washington National Cathedral. The final finial sits atop the southwest pinnacle of the cathedral's southwest tower, and the long-serving Linden crane has retreated. As the program on the ground was completed, and Pres. George H.W. Bush was whisked off to other presidential business, Washington National Cathedral moved into a new era. In the time since its completion, members of the community at Washington National Cathedral have endeavored to make their special church a spiritual home for the United States and a world religious site. (Photograph by Susan Jensen.)

WASHINGTON NATIONAL CATHEDRAL. On completion, Washington National Cathedral became the largest completed entirely masonry building on the North American continent. It contains, inside and out, what must be the most astounding collections of 20th-century carved stone, stained glass, carved wood, ornamental wrought iron, and needlepoint to be found anywhere in the world. Following the cathedral's completion, a team of economic historians was convened, provided with all the completed and paid contracts, and asked to make an attempt at adjusting all the expenditures to the value of a 1990 dollar. The results of these studies all fell within a $3 million range, placing the final cost of building Washington National Cathedral's fabric at somewhere between $62 and $65 million. In the decade following the cathedral's completion, the entire building was wired-up and watched, electronically, for all the shifting, moving, and settlement one might expect in a masonry building of such size. The finding of the study determined that, as long as mankind or earthquakes do not knock Washington National Cathedral down, it should stand, without further reinforcement, for the better part of the next two millennia. (Photograph by Carol M. Highsmith, LOC.)

Visit us at
arcadiapublishing.com

....